GAMES STUDENTS LIKE TO PLAY

GAMES STUDENTS LIKE TO PLAY

Games and Activities for
Elementary School
Junior High School
Senior High School

JOHN WILLIAM BENSON
Garfield High School
Los Angeles City Schools

Fearon Publishers
Belmont, California

To my wonderful mother and father.

ISBN-0-8224-3270-6

Printed in the United States of America.

Contents

PREFACE   vii

GAMES FOR INTRODUCING A LESSON   1

    Crossword Puzzle, 2

    Treasure Hunt, 4

    Dig, 6

    Track, 8

    Faces, 9

    Hollywood Squares, 12

    The Match Game, 13

GAMES FOR REVIEWING A LESSON   15

    Around the World, 16

    Competitive Seating Chart, 17

    Baseball, 18

    Basketball, 19

    Football, 21

    Golf, 26

    Roller Derby, 28

    Concentration, 30

    Eye Guess, 33

    Historingo, 36

    Jeopardy, 37

    Password, 40

    Personality, 41

To Tell the Truth, 42

Truth or Consequences, 43

Twenty Questions, 43

You Don't Say, 44

Preface

Both first-year teachers and old pros will welcome the change of pace these games can bring to the classroom. The activities have been used most successfully in eight years of practical application and can easily be adapted to meet the needs of students at the elementary, junior high, and senior high school levels.

The intent of this book is to aid the teacher in bringing variety and fun into the classroom, on the premise that if education is made attractive and enjoyable, the student will be highly motivated to learn. There are other advantages to this approach—an informal but well-ordered atmosphere, conducive to maximum learning, prevails in the game-oriented classroom. Also, the student who is highly motivated does not present a discipline problem because he disciplines himself; as a result, order comes from the students and not from the teacher.

Many teachers are at a loss when it comes to employing different techniques in their classrooms. The general pattern is one of introduction, lecture and discussion, review, testing, and an occasional follow-up activity. This book contains a number of techniques that can be used to break the routine, and create enjoyment and excitement in learning. The games do not have to be read in the order presented—simply turn through the pages and choose the ones that appeal to you.

You'll find that most of the activities in this book will be familiar to both you and your students. Almost everybody has, at one time or another, worked a crossword puzzle, seen a football game, or watched Jeopardy on television. The rules of the games are, therefore, generally well known, even though they now will be used in a different setting.

These games have an unusually wide range of application. They work well with both accelerated and slow students, whether in homogeneous or heterogeneous groupings. In addition, these games can be adapted to almost any subject. Social science illustrations are used exclusively in this book only because the author is a social science teacher. By retaining the game structure but using different subject matter, the games have infinite versatility.

Finally, these activities are also economical. The teacher does not have to invest a small fortune in equipment because the games cost little or nothing to construct. And more important, little time is required to prepare the activities.

The procedures and rules detailed in the book are the result of much experimentation and revision. But to place restrictions on the teacher's creativity would be foolhardy. It is hoped that the reader will improvise on the games to fit his own classroom needs.

John William Benson

Games for
Introducing a Lesson

CROSSWORD PUZZLE

OBJECTIVE: To answer definitions or incomplete sentences and to fit these answers into a crossword puzzle.

HOW TO PLAY: Give each student a dittoed sheet of paper with a crossword diagram and a list of questions. The bottom portion of this puzzle lists descriptive clues, some needing sentence completion, after a series of numbers. (The answers appear in parentheses.) The numbers tell the student how many letters are in each answer. For example, the first question is preceded by the number 4 and the answer is Marx, a four-letter word.

Students find the answers through individual research, then fit the answers into the puzzle. The best way to do this is to start with the word that intercepts the base word—RUSSIA, in this case. The puzzle tells us that the first letter of this nine-letter word begins with an "S." The only nine-letter word beginning with "S" on the list is socialism, so the student enters that word in the proper spaces. The second "i" of socialism now becomes the ninth letter of an eleven-letter word. The rest of the puzzle is worked by repeating this process.

When a number of students have completed the puzzle, ask one of them to put it on the chalkboard, then discuss each answer with the class. This type of puzzle can be used as a launching pad for class discussions and has the added virtue of giving the slower students a sense of accomplishment. The completed crossword puzzle also serves as a ready-made study guide for the student.

Spaces	Clues

4	"Father of Communism"; wrote <u>Capital</u> and the Communist Manifesto. (Marx)
6	Helped write the Communist Manifesto; a friend of Marx. (Engels)
7	This book is considered the "bible of communism." (<u>Capital</u>)
8	Where the word "communism" comes from. (Communis)
9	System where government owns everything; take power peacefully. (socialism)
	System where government owns everything; take power with force. (communism)
	"Communist _____", book written by two men. (Manifesto)
10	Name for larger group of Social Democrats. (Bolsheviki)
11	Marx's word for the working class. (proletariat)
	Marx's word for the upper class. (bourgeoisie)
12	Two words: Value of product equals labor required to produce it. (surplus value)
13	Two words: Clash of interests between owners and wage workers. (class struggle)

CONSTRUCTION: Browse through the material you wish to introduce and write key words on a plain piece of paper. Then, using graph paper, juggle these words so that one letter of one word becomes one letter of another word.

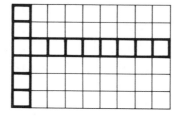

When all of the key words have been inserted into the puzzle, place the graph paper on top of a ditto master and clip the two sheets together. Using a ruler and a pencil, blacken the squares around the letters. Be sure to press hard.

Next, separate the two sheets of paper. Keep the graph paper as your answer sheet. Place the ditto master in a typewriter and type the base word, then the questions. Arrange the words from shortest to longest. In front of each question, type the number of letters that are in the answer. Run off the ditto master and your puzzle is complete.

TREASURE HUNT

OBJECTIVE: To answer definitions or incomplete sentences, to fit these answers into a crossword puzzle, and ultimately to uncover the mystery saying.

HOW TO PLAY: Give each student a dittoed sheet of paper with a cross-word diagram and a list of questions. Direct them to fill in the puzzle with the answers to the questions. Then have them fill in the blanks in the mystery saying with letters from squares with corresponding numbers. The slashes (/) indicate the ends of words. The numeral in front of each question indicates the number of letters in the answer.

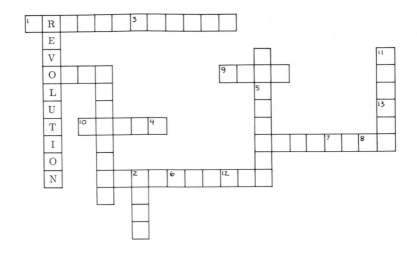

Spaces	Clues

4	The "Father of Communism"; wrote <u>Capital</u>. (Marx)
	Nickname given to Lenin's followers in the Civil War. (Reds)
	Key industrial city west of the Urals. (Omsk)
5	Father of the 1917 Russian Revolution; sent by the Germans. (Lenin)
6	Nickname given to the enemies of Lenin in the Civil War. (Whites)
7	Great organizer for Lenin in the Civil War. (Trotsky)
8	Attempted to bring democracy to Russia with his Provisional Government. (Kerensky)
	The First Secretary of the Communist Party in Russia in 1973. (Brezhnev)
	Last Russian Czar; abdicated in 1917. (Nicholas)
10	The last Russian to hold the two main offices in Russia at the same time; he left power in 1964. (Khrushchev)
12	Place where Germany and Russia signed treaty pulling Russia out of World War I. (Brest Litovsk)

$$\underline{\ }\ \underline{\ }\ \underline{\ }\ \underline{G}\ / \quad \underline{\ }\ \underline{\ }\ \underline{\ }\ \underline{\ }\ \underline{\ }\ / \quad \underline{\ }\ / \quad \underline{\ }\ \underline{\ }\ \underline{\ }\ \underline{P}\ \underline{\ }\ / \quad \underline{\ }\ \underline{F}\ /$$
$$\quad 1\ 2\ 3\ 4 \qquad\quad 1\ 5\ 4\ 6\ 7\ 4 \qquad 8 \qquad 6\ 8\ 9\ 10\ 5 \qquad 7$$

$$\underline{\ }\ \underline{\ }\ \underline{\ }\ \underline{\ }\ / \quad \underline{\ }\ \underline{U}\ \underline{\ }\ \underline{\ }\ \underline{\ }\ / \quad \underline{\ }\ \underline{\ }\ / \quad \underline{\ }\ \underline{\ }\ \underline{\ }\ \underline{-}\ \underline{\ }\ \underline{\ }\ \underline{\ }\ \underline{D}\ / \quad \underline{\ }\ \underline{F}.$$
$$11\ 12\ 8\ 13 \qquad 2\quad 6\ 6\ 3\ 8 \qquad 12\ 8\ 6 \qquad 7\ 4\ 5\ 13\ 12\ 3\ 2 \qquad 7$$

The first portion of this paper is worked in the same manner as a regular crossword puzzle (see pages 2 and 3). Selected squares, however, contain numbers. The letter that falls in the square numbered 1, for example, should be written in the corresponding blank in the mystery saying. In this case, the letter that falls in square number 1 is "B" from "Brest Litovsk." The mystery saying for this puzzle is: BRING BENSON A SAMPLE OF WHAT RUSSIA HAS ONE-THIRD OF. It calls for the student to leave the room and bring the teacher a sample of what Russia has one-third of. If the student can remember the fact that Russia has one-third of the world's forests, he goes out in search of a sample of a tree. The first student to return to class with a twig, leaf, or piece of bark is the winner.

CONSTRUCTION: This puzzle is made in the same way as the regular crossword puzzle (see page 4).

To add the mystery saying to the puzzle, refer to the graph paper containing the completed puzzle. At the bottom of the graph paper write a saying that incorporates many of the letters in the puzzle.

Take the first letter of the first word in the saying and locate the same letter in the puzzle. Write the number 1 in that box in the puzzle and write the number 1 beneath all letters in the saying that correspond to the letter in the box.

If some letters in the saying cannot be found in the puzzle, type them in the saying in the appropriate place with no number beneath them.

After the entire saying has been numbered, type it onto a ditto master, run off the master, and you are ready to play.

DIG

OBJECTIVE: To answer a list of questions and to uncover the mystery saying.

HOW TO PLAY: Give each student a dittoed sheet of paper, similar to the one on the next page.

The student begins by reading the chapter under study and filling in the missing words. When all the blanks have been filled, the student can figure out the mystery saying.

To arrive at the saying, use two sets of numbers. The example says "1 of answer to 4." The first number tells you which letter to use, and the second number tells you which answer to use. In this case, you use the first letter of answer number 4. Place this letter in the first blank.

The next set of numbers involves the letter to be placed in the second dash and so on. Thus, as you move down the set of numbers, you are filling in the blanks from left to right.

Chapter 3

1. This organization, formed in 1885, was not a legislative body, but a Hindu political organization. _____ _____ _____ (Indian National Congress)

2. This organization was formed in 1906 by Aga Khan to compete with the Hindu organization. _____ _____ _____ _____ (All India Moslem League)

3. In World War I the Indians made important contributions to the _____ war effort. (British)

4. This President of the United States said the world war was fought "to make the world safe for democracy." (Last name) _____ (Wilson)

5. This man has been called the George Washington of India. (Last name) _____ (Gandhi)

6. English translation of Mahatma, Gandhi's nickname. _____ _____ (Great Soul)

7. Gandhi's basic policy was ahimsa, or _____. (non-violence)

8. Gandhi, first and foremost, wanted _____ for India. (freedom)

9. Gandhi launched a campaign of _____ _____. (civil disobedience)

10. Winston Churchill was defeated in 1945 by the Labor Party, which now formed a government headed by _____ (Last name). (Attlee)

11. This country was created for the Moslems. _____ (Pakistan)

12. _____ (Last name) was leader of the Moslem League and first governor general of Pakistan. (Jinnah)

1 of answer to 4
6 & 5 of answer to 12
5 of first word in answer 6
* * *
5 & 6 of answer to 3
* * *
6 of answer to 11
5 of answer to 5
5 of answer to 10
* * *
1 of third word to answer 2
2 & 6 of answer to 5
1 of answer to 7
* * *

1 of first word to answer 9
2 & 6 of answer to 8
1 of answer to 11
* * *
4 & 5 of third word to answer 1
6 of answer to 8
1 & 6 of answer to 4
* * *
2 & 3 of answer to 12
* * *
6 of answer to 5
3 of answer to 12
4 & 6 of answer to 5
1 of answer to 10
* * *

_ _ _ _/ _ _/ _ _ _/ _ _ _ _/ _ _ _ _/ _ _ _ _ _/

_ _/ _ _ _ _ _?

TRACK

OBJECTIVE: To score more points than the opposing teams.

HOW TO PLAY: Track is an introduction to the school library and should only be employed the first time the class visits the library.

Divide the class into three or four teams of similar ability. When the class meets in the library, seat each team together as shown.

```
X X X X                          Y Y Y Y
   1                                2
X X X X        Teacher           Y Y Y Y
               W X Y Z
W W W W                          Z Z Z Z
   3                                4
W W W W                          Z Z Z Z
```

Call for the first member of each team to stand next to the teacher. Refer to a set of questions dealing with various information that can be located in the library. (Prepare these questions ahead of time.)

Sample questions

1. Bring me a book of fiction written by an author whose last name begins with the letter "S. "
2. Bring me a book on China.
3. Bring me a political cartoon.
4. In what year was Gandhi born?
5. Bring me a magazine article about Mao Tse-Tung. Use the Reader's Guide to Periodical Literature.
6. Bring me an autobiography.
7. Compile a bibliography of seven sources concerning Stalin.
8. Bring me a pamphlet about the United Nations.
9. Show me a historical map of post-World War I Europe.
10. Bring me a biography of a contemporary personality.

Read the first question aloud. The four students then attempt to locate the necessary information as quickly as possible. The first student to locate the material and show it to the teacher wins that race and scores five points for his team. The second-place student scores three points, and the third student scores one point. When the race is over, discuss the question and ask the participants where they went to get the necessary information.

For the next race, call on a new student from each team. No student may race twice until every other member of his team has participated in one race.

At the end of the period, total the points for each team. The winner is the team with the most points.

Given a good assortment of questions, the students will gain an appreciation for the astounding variety of information that can be located in the school library.

FACES

OBJECTIVE: To recognize the faces of famous people.

HOW TO PLAY: On the bulletin board, clearly visible to the entire class, pin up a set of six numbered cards.

○	1	○
○	2	○
○	3	○
○	4	○
○	5	○
○	6	○

On the reverse side of these cards, in jumbled order, appear pieces of the picture of a famous person that is pertinent to the lesson. The teacher acts as a moderator. First, call on a student, then read a question orally. Because they are used to introduce a new area, the questions should be general in nature.

If the student gives a correct response, ask him which card he would like to have turned over, thereby exposing a portion of the person's face. If the student asks that card 4 be turned over, the result might be as shown on the next page.

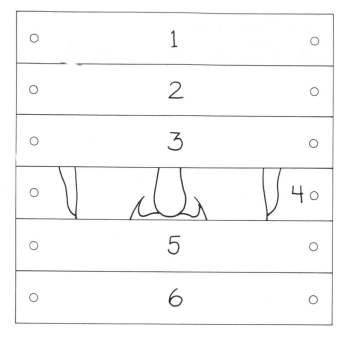

Next, ask the student who answered the question correctly if he can identify the person. If the student answers correctly, the game is over. If the student does not know the answer or gives an incorrect identification, ask the next student a different question.

If the initial question was answered incorrectly by the first student, ask any other student who raises his hand the same question. If he gives a correct answer, follow the procedure outlined above. If an incorrect answer is given the second time, the teacher gives the correct answer and moves on to another question and another student.

If all of the cards have been turned over and the person has not yet been identified, continue to ask questions in the manner outlined above. When a correct answer is given, that student can switch any two cards. For example, the student might wish to exchange cards 2 and 4 in the example on the next page.

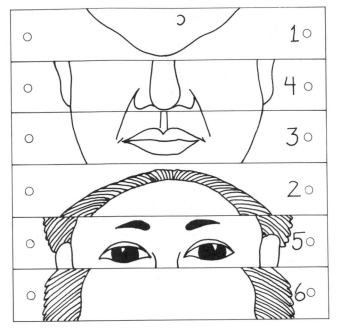

If all of the cards have been maneuvered so that the picture is in order, and still no one knows who the person is, the teacher identifies the individual and the game is over.

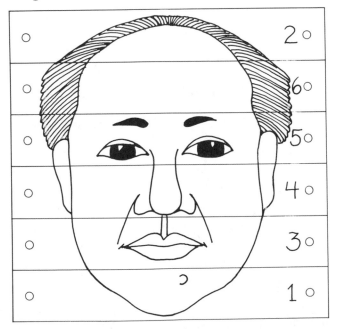

CONSTRUCTION: Pin a large piece of construction paper on your bulletin board. Obtain a picture of the person you want the students to identify. Place the picture in an opaque projector and aim the reflected image so that it covers the construction paper. Pencil the reflected image onto the construction paper. Go over the pencil marks with a dark felt-tip pen so that the picture can be seen easily from a distance. The drawing can be made freehand, but accuracy counts. It is most important that the final drawing clearly resemble the individual in question. When the drawing is complete, take the construction paper from the bulletin board and lay it on a flat surface. Using a ruler, divide the picture horizontally into six (or more) equal divisions. Then cut it along the penciled lines.

Take one of the cards and punch holes in both sides of it. Then place the punched card over another card, clip the two together, and punch the second card. When all of the cards have been punched, lay the cards down, face up in a mixed order. Using a felt-tip pen, write one number per card on either the extreme left or right side so that it does not obstruct the picture. Turn the cards over and print the same number on the back. You are now ready to pin the cards in numerical order on the bulletin board.

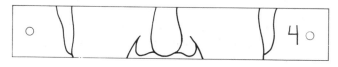

Write a large number of easy questions from the new area of study and you are ready to play. This game is a wonderful way to start a new semester by measuring how much students know about a new unit.

HOLLYWOOD SQUARES

OBJECTIVE: To fill in three consecutive squares (vertically, horizontally, or diagonally) with X's or O's.

HOW TO PLAY: Seat nine students in the form of a tic-tac-toe board, then draw a tic-tac-toe diagram on the chalkboard.

```
O   O   O   O   O

O   X   X   X   O

O   X   X   X   O

O   X   X   X   O
```

Seating arrangement: X represents students forming tic-tac-toe board.

Diagram to be drawn on chalkboard.

Select two students to come to the front of the room and sit down facing the class. Name one student "X, " the other "O. "

Let the "X" student begin. Ask him where he would like to place his first X. He looks at the diagram on the board and picks his square. Let's say that he picks the middle square. The teacher then picks the student who corresponds to that square. (The X on the chalkboard corresponds to X in the seating arrangement.) The teacher then asks a question of student X. When student X gives his answer, the "X" student in the front of the room must state whether the answer was correct or incorrect.

If X gave a correct answer and "X" said it was a correct answer, or if X gave an incorrect answer and "X" said it was incorrect, X wins the square. An X is then drawn in the middle square of the diagram on the chalkboard. The "O" student in front of the room now follows the same procedure, designating where he wants to place his mark.

If, on the other hand, X gave a correct answer and "X" said it was incorrect, or X gave an incorrect answer and "X" said it was correct, X does not get the square and "O" takes a turn.

The "X" and "O" players continue rotating until one of them has been awarded three consecutive squares horizontally, vertically, or diagonally. Whichever player does this first is declared the winner, or else the game is over when all of the squares have been won without either player getting three in a row. In this case, O is the winner because there are more O's than X's.

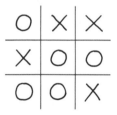

Because new material is being introduced, use multiple-choice questions. Ask all the students to take notes on the questions and correct responses.

THE MATCH GAME

OBJECTIVE: To have several students in one row write the same word in response to a word verbally given by the teacher.

HOW TO PLAY: Divide the class into four or five teams of equal number. Instruct all students to take out a piece of paper and a pencil or pen.

Read the class a word that pertains to the new area of study (for example, if Africa is the new area, the word might be "jungle").

All students then write down the first word that comes to their minds in response to "jungle." Quickly check all of the students' responses, team by team. If two students on the same team wrote the same word, that team scores one point. If three students in the same team have matching words, that team gets two points. If four students wrote matching answers, that team receives three points. And if all five answers match, that team wins four points.

Record the scores on the chalkboard, then discuss the original word as it relates to the new area of study.

Repeat this procedure using other words. The team that scores the most points by the end of the game is declared the winner.

Games for
Reviewing a Lesson

AROUND THE WORLD

OBJECTIVE: To answer questions more rapidly than an opponent and work toward a seat in the "payoff chair" at one end of the room.

HOW TO PLAY: Instruct the students to change their seating so that all chairs on one side of the room are occupied:

```
O   O   X   X   X   X

O   O   X   X   X   X

O   O   X   X   X   X

O   O   X   X   X   X

O   X   X   X   X   X
```

O = unoccupied chairs
X = occupied chairs

Take out a set of index cards, each containing a question with a short answer. Ask the students to take out their notes and a blank sheet of paper to take additional notes.

Walk over to one side of the room and instruct X1 to take his notes and stand next to X2, as follows:

```
O   O   X   X   X   X

O   O   X   X   X   X

O   O   X   X   X   X3

O   O   X   X   X   X2  X1

O   X   X   X   X        ↗    Teacher
```

Play begins as you read the first question aloud so that it can be heard throughout the room. X1 and X2 are the only ones who may answer the question, either from memory or by referring to notes. The first one to correctly answer the question moves on to challenge X3, and the loser sits down in X2's chair.

If neither student can give a correct answer within ten seconds, call time and read the answer orally. Then give the same students a new question. If both students give a correct response simultaneously, you'll need to give them another question to break the tie.

The movement of the challenges follows the path of the arrow in the following chart. The object is for the students to work their way into the chair occupied by X4.

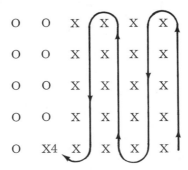

The chair occupied by X4 is the payoff chair. A reward (such as points on the next examination) is given to the student who is sitting in this chair when the game is over.

When a challenger arrives to contest X4 for his chair, a different procedure is followed. Because the payoff chair is the last chair, the loser of this contest must start from the beginning position (X2 because X1's chair is no longer occupied) and attempt to work his way around the world again.

This is such a rapid-paced game that the teacher will travel around the room many times, allowing many students to eventually contest for the payoff chair.

Because so many questions can be covered in this game, it is wise to have a large number of them written on separate index cards (no less than 50 is recommended). When all the questions have been exhausted, use them again, possibly changing the wording the second time around.

COMPETITIVE SEATING CHART

OBJECTIVE: To allow one student to challenge another for the right to sit in the challenged student's chair.

HOW TO PLAY: One day a week, usually on a Friday or the following Monday, set a portion of the period aside to allow students to change their seating arrangement. The wish to change is recognized when one student challenges an adjacent student for that student's chair. The position diagram on the next page shows the possible challenges a student may make.

```
O   O   O   O   O

O   X   X   X   O

O   X   *   X   O

O   X   X   X   O

O   O   O   O   O
```

* = challenger
X = chairs that may be challenged
O = chairs that cannot be chal-
 lenged immediately

The challenger and challenged are asked a maximum of seven questions, dealing with work covered during that week which involve short
answers (for example: Who is the Father of Radio? Lee deForest). The
teacher reads the first question and whichever student gives the correct
answer first wins one round. The first one to win four rounds is declared the winner.

If the challenger wins four out of seven rounds, he has won the right
to sit in the challenged student's chair. He may continue to challenge
adjacent students until he is defeated. Then he must wait until the following week to resume his attempts.

If the challenged student wins the four rounds first, he remains in
his chair and has the opportunity of challenging any adjacent student.
The game ends when no student wants to challenge another.

Because most students dislike seating charts, this activity provides
an opportunity for them to exchange seats often and motivates them to
review weekly the work covered in class.

BASEBALL

OBJECTIVE: To score more runs than the opposing team.

HOW TO PLAY: This game is played like regular baseball, except that
the batter is the student, the ball is the question, the hit or homerun is
the correct answer, the out is the incorrect answer, and the pitcher is
the teacher.

Divide the class into two teams of similar ability. Seat one team on
one side of the room, the other team on the other side. Draw the following diagram on the chalkboard:

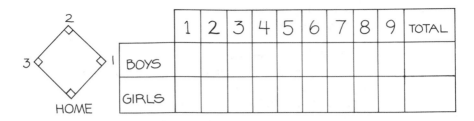

	1	2	3	4	5	6	7	8	9	TOTAL
BOYS										
GIRLS										

The visiting team (boys) goes to bat first. The first student on that team asks the pitcher (teacher) for a single, double, triple, or homerun question. The better the hit requested, the harder will be the question.

Single: What is the capital city of Russia?
           How does Russia rank with the other countries of the world in land size?

Double: Give two prominent characteristics of the Taiga belt.

Triple: Chernozem is found in the Steppe belt. What is chernozem?

Homerun: Give five major causes which led to the downfall of Czar Nicholas II.

Let's suppose a single hit question is requested. If the student answers it correctly, draw an X on first base and the next batter (student) steps up to the plate. An incorrect answer equals one out. After three outs, the other team goes to bat.

To score a run, a team must answer four single questions or any other appropriate combination (a triple and single question, two double questions, one homerun, and so on) before recording three outs in any one inning. Runs may be scored in one inning until the three outs have been recorded.

Play a nine-inning game, or play until the period ends. Record the score inning by inning on the chalkboard. The team with the most runs is the winner.

BASKETBALL

OBJECTIVE: To make more baskets than the opponent team.

HOW TO PLAY: Divide the class into two teams of similar ability and seat them on opposite sides of the room. Choose one student to keep score on the chalkboard. Instruct the students to take out their notes and a blank sheet of paper for taking additional notes.

Play begins with a jump ball. Ask the first player from each team to come to the front of the room, then read a short-answer question.

The first student to give the correct answer wins the jump ball, and his team takes possession of the ball. Both students then return to their chairs.

The team that has the ball may now try to score a basket (two points). Ask the second student on that team whether he would like to shoot for a basket or pass the ball to a teammate.

If the student prefers to make a basket, read him a question. If he answers it correctly, his team wins two points and the ball goes to the other team.

If no answer is given, or if the answer is incorrect, anyone in the room may attempt to claim the "rebound" and get possession of the ball for his team by raising his hand first, being recognized by the teacher, and giving the correct answer. If no student answers the question, the teacher calls for a jump ball to determine who takes possession. The student who is asked the question first cannot refer to any notes, but all other students may.

If the ball is passed to a second player, however, the first player is asked the same question as if he were scoring a basket. If he gives the correct answer, he then passes the ball to a teammate and that player now chooses whether he would like to make a basket or pass the ball again. If an incorrect answer is given on an attempted pass, a turnover results. No points are awarded and the other team gets possession of the ball.

Unless the ball is passed, the teacher interrogates the students in order, going up one row and down the other (after student 1 of team 1 and student 1 of team 2 score, it is now student 2 of team 1's turn).

The advantage of passing the ball over making a basket is that the set order may be broken. If student 2 of team 1 knows that student 3 of his team is unfamiliar with the material under review, he can pass the ball to student 4, thereby preventing student 3 of his team from being questioned by the teacher.

Another advantage of passing the ball is that a team with only a few knowledgeable students can stall (pass the ball back and forth to teammates and waste time) and possibly defeat a team of more informed students. The disadvantage of passing is that an incorrect answer gives the ball directly to the other team.

Divide the game into two halves of equal time (approximately 20 minutes per half). Begin the second half with a jump ball. The team that has scored more points at the end of the second half is declared the winner.

FOOTBALL

OBJECTIVE: To move the ball down the field and score a touchdown.

HOW TO PLAY: Draw a football field on the chalkboard.

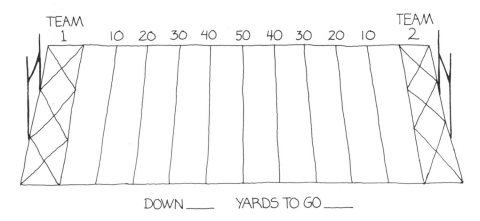

Team 1's score is recorded in the upper left corner, and Team 2's score goes in the upper right corner. Divide the class into two teams of similar ability. Seat Team 1 on one side of the room, Team 2 on the other side. Instruct the students to take out their notes and a blank sheet of paper for taking additional notes.

Appoint one member of each team to act as captain. Ask the two captains to come to the front of the room. (The teacher, acting as the referee, introduces the two captains to one another and tells them to shake hands.) Instruct one of the captains to call heads or tails as you flip the coin in the air. The captain who wins the toss then has the option of kicking or receiving to begin the game. Both captains then return to their seats.

Suppose that the captain of Team 1 wins the toss and elects to receive the kickoff. In this case, you would instruct the captain of Team 2 to kickoff by choosing a number between 1 and 10. The teacher holds a card labeled "kickoffs" with a list of ten numbers appearing on that card. Beside each number is listed one situation that might occur; the same is true for the punt card. See the sample kickoff and punt cards on the next page.

When a number is called, check that number and do not use it again. Suppose that Team 2's captain selects the number 3. Read the situation that appears following the number 3 on the card: the ball was kicked in the end zone and will be placed on the 20-yard line. Choose a student to draw a picture of a football on the 20-yard line of the diagram on the chalkboard. This student can also serve as scorekeeper.

Kickoffs

1. onside to 50-yard line—successful
2. to 20—returned 20 yards
3. end zone—on 20-yard line
4. to 5—returned 40 yards
5. unsuccessful onside—own 40-yard line
6. end zone—on 20-yard line
7. to 15—returned 10 yards
8. to 25—returned 40 yards
9. end zone—on 20-yard line
10. onside to 50-yard line—successful

Punts

1. blocked
2. 40 yards—returned 10 yards
3. 60 yards—no return
4. fake—gain 25 yards
5. 30 yards—returned 40 yards
6. fake—lose 5 yards
7. 60 yards—returned 10 yards
8. blocked
9. 45 yards—no return
10. 50 yards—returned 35 yards

The object of the game from this point on is the same as in regular football: to advance the ball down the field by gaining first downs (10 yards in a maximum of four attempts) and eventually to reach the opponent's end zone and score a touchdown (six points). This is done in the following manner.

First, ask the first student of Team 1 whether he would like to go for 5 yards, 10 yards, or 30 yards. To gain 5 yards the student will be required to answer a question of minimum difficulty; the 10-yard questions will be more difficult; and the 30-yard questions will be those of greatest difficulty.

Let's suppose that the first student of Team 1 selects a 5-yard question. Take out three sets of cards: 5-yard questions (easy), 10-yard questions (difficult), and 30-yard questions (very difficult). See the sample question cards on the next page.

5 yards

What is the Moslem holy book called?

Koran

---

10 yards

Who are five of the six main Moslem prophets?

Adam, Noah, Abraham, Moses, Jesus, and Mohammed

---

30 yards

List and describe the Five Pillars of Islam.

Daily recitation of creed, prayer five times daily, fast during Ramadan, almsgiving, and pilgrimage to Mecca once in a lifetime.

Question cards

To compensate for the degree of difficulty in the three sets of questions, a maximum of 10 seconds should be allowed for answering the 5-yard questions, 20 seconds for the 10-yard questions, and one to three minutes for tho 30-yard questions.

Because a 5-yard question was requested in this case, take the first question in the 5-yard stack and read it aloud to the class. The student who asked for the question then has 10 seconds to give the correct answer (without referring to his notes). If the student gives the answer within the 10-second time limit, the ball is moved forward five yards to that team's 25-yard line. It now becomes second down with five yards to go for a first down. If another 5-yard question is answered within three more downs, the ball would be drawn on the 30-yard line, and that team would have four more attempts to gain another first down and retain possession, thus moving the ball towards the opponent's end zone.

If, on the other hand, the student who is asked the original question is unable to give an answer in the 10-second time limit, the teacher calls time. This call indicates that Team 1 has fumbled. Any member of either team who knows the answer, either by memory or by reviewing his notes, may raise his hand as soon as time is called. Call on the first student who raised his hand. If that student was a member of the team that fumbled the ball and he gives a correct answer, Team 1 has recovered its own fumble, the ball remains on the 20-yard line, and it now becomes second down and 10 yards to go for the first down. But if a student from Team 2 raises his hand first and gives a correct answer, Team 2 recovers the fumble and is only 20 yards from a touchdown.

Finally, if the original student being asked the question gives an incorrect answer, this also constitutes a fumble. As soon as the wrong answer is given, any member of either team may raise his hand to attempt to recover the fumble for his team, following the procedures described above.

Each team is allowed one chance to recover every fumble. If a recovery does not occur (if no one knows the correct answer), Team 1 retains possession but loses the down. Consequently it now becomes second down and 10 yards to go for the first down.

If Team 1 has not made a first down and it is fourth down and 5 or 10 yards to go for a first down, the student whose turn it is to answer a question has the option of going for the necessary yardage or punting. If that student makes the necessary yardage by correctly answering the question, Team 1 keeps possession of the ball; if that student goes for the yardage unsuccessfully, by either incorrectly answering the question or giving no answer, Team 2 takes possession of the ball. If the student decides to punt, follow the same procedure used in kickoffs, but refer to the card labeled "punts" instead.

When you ask the students questions, do not call on them at random, but go up one row and down the other so that all students have an opportunity to play. If a team fumbles and later recovers another fumble, question the student whose turn it would have been had the original fumble not occurred.

Divide the game into two halves of equal time. No matter where the ball is located on the field at the end of the first half, the second half begins with a kickoff by the team that received to start the game. Kickoffs also follow all touchdowns.

Optional Circumstances

1. Extra points following touchdowns. To make the game more interesting, one- and two-point conversions may be used following touchdowns. Ask the student who scored the touchdown whether he would like to go for one or two points. The single extra point would require him to answer a 5-yard question, whereas the two-point conversion would call for a 10-yard question. Failure to meet the time limit or an incorrect answer would mean an unsuccessful attempt with no extra point(s) being awarded and no fumble recoveries allowed. Conversion attempts, whether successful or not, are followed by a kickoff by the team that has just scored.

2. Field goals. A 3-point field goal might be used, to be attempted from anywhere inside the opponent's 50-yard line. To see that field goals are tried discriminately, they should involve the answering of 30-yard questions. If the field goal is successful, it is followed by a kickoff. If the attempt fails (that is, if the question is answered incorrectly), the ball is placed on the opposing team's 20-yard line, and that team gains possession with a first down and 10 yards to go for a first down.

3. Time outs. Time outs may be used for strategy purposes. Grant each team one one-minute time out per each half. This time out could be used strategically to prevent the opposing team from scoring at the end of either half.

Suppose that the score is 7-0 in favor of Team 1, but Team 2 has the ball on Team 1's 5-yard line with one minute remaining in the game. Team 1 may call time out, and time will expire before Team 2 gets another chance to put the ball in play.

4. Penalties. Various penalties might be employed to control student conduct, such as illegal use of the mouth (5 yards) for giving answers to a teammate, or excessive talking.

GOLF

OBJECTIVE: To take fewer "shots" (giving an answer to various clues) than the opponent team.

HOW TO PLAY: Divide the class into two (or more) teams of similar ability. Have Team 1 sit in a circle on one side of the room; Team 2 follows the same seating arrangement on the other side of the room. (If more than two teams are playing, place them in different corners of the room.) Write the numbers from 1 to 18 in one column on the blackboard, and beside it make columns for scoring Teams 1 and 2.

```
                X   X   X   X   X
            X                       X
            X                       X       Team 1
                X   X   X   X   X

Teacher

                O   O   O   O   O
            O                       O
            O                       O       Team 2
                O   O   O   O   O
```

The teacher needs a set of 18 cards, one card per hole. Each card contains an answer and three clues to help the students arrive at that answer. The first clue is very difficult; the second creates greater understanding; and the third should lead to the desired answer. If an 18-hole round is to be played, as in regular golf, 18 different cards will be required.

Hole #1

1. A fisherman and woman could both make use of this object. (net)

2. Name for a yellow car with a meter. (cab)

3. Name of the group of top Presidential advisers.

CABINET

To begin the game, pick up the card labeled hole #1 and read the first clue appearing on that card. This is a difficult clue that will probably not produce the correct answer. It corresponds to the first shot ("tee" shot) in regular golf. Seldom does anyone make a hole-in-one.

After the first clue is given, each team has one minute to conduct an open, quiet discussion about the clue. All students are encouraged to look at their notes and books for possible answers. One spokesman for each team is designated to write each answer after the discussions for the teacher to view.

If both teams give the correct answer on the first clue (which rarely happens), each team scores a hole-in-one and the number 1 is written next to hole #1 on the chalkboard under each team's name.

If Team 1 gives a correct answer but Team 2 does not, Team 1 is credited with a hole-in-one while Team 2 is now ready to take its second shot (receive its second clue). If it gives the correct answer following the second clue, Team 2 scores a two on that hole. If the third clue is needed because an incorrect answer followed the second one, that team will have one more opportunity to guess the answer. The third clue should lead to the correct answer and, therefore, it corresponds to "par" in regular golf, par being defined as the number of shots it should take an average golfer to complete the hole.

If Team 2 still fails to give the correct answer after clue three is given, Team 2 is credited with scoring a bogey (one over par) or four points on the hole.

A one-minute discussion follows each clue and is only allowed to the team that has not yet completed the hole. In the discussion, reference can be made to books or notes.

Each of the remaining holes is played in the same manner. When the course is completed, the scores of each team are added. On the next page is a sample score card.

The team with the lowest total (Team 2 in this case) is declared the winner.

Hole	Team 1	Team 2
1	1	1
2	3	2
3	4	3
4	2	3
5	3	3
6	3	4
7	3	3
8	3	3
9	2	2
10	3	2
11	3	3
12	4	4
13	2	3
14	2	1
15	3	3
16	3	2
17	4	4
18	2	3
Total:	50	49

ROLLER DERBY

OBJECTIVE: To score more points than the opposing team.

HOW TO PLAY: Divide the class into two teams of similar ability, then divide each team into a girls and boys team, with a minimum of five students each.

Seat the five girls of one team in one row (at desks or on the floor) and the five boys of that team in an adjoining row. Follow this seating arrangement for the other team on the other side of the room. Seat all the other students (substitutes) in the middle rows. Select one student to be the timer; he sits at the front of room. The teacher acts as the referee. The final class arrangement looks like this:

```
                    X  X  X  X  X     Girls
          Team 1    O  O  O  O  O     Boys
   Timer            S  S  S  S  S     Substitutes

   Teacher          S  S  S  S  S     Substitutes
          Team 2    O  O  O  O  O     Boys
                    X  X  X  X  X     Girls
```

The game begins with either Team 1 boys versus Team 2 boys or Team 1 girls versus Team 2 girls. Points scored by both the boys and girls of one team will be counted as a part of the entire team's total score.

Let's suppose that the girls teams will begin the game. They will have six minutes (one period) in which to score as many points as they can for their respective teams. When the six minutes are over, the timer calls time and the boys' teams then play for a six-minute period. The teams will rotate like this every six minutes until the game ends. Each six-minute period is broken into one-and-a-half minute "jam" (scoring) periods. Points may be scored only during these periods.

If the girls are going to start the game, they arrange their seating strategically, so that the more knowledgeable girls are located at the front and back of their row. When they are ready, ask the girls seated at the front of their respective rows to stand. They will determine who will become the "jammer" (scorer).

Referring to a set of questions involving short answers (for example: Under the Articles of Confederation, how many branches of government were established? One legislative.), ask the two girls a question. The first girl to answer the question becomes the scorer (although no points have yet been scored), and the other girl returns to her seat.

If both girls give the correct answer simultaneously, or if neither one knows the answer, continue asking questions until one girl beats the other. She then has one-and-a-half minutes to attempt to score a maximum of five points by passing each member of the opposing girls' team, including the unsuccessful jammer.

The scorer circles the room until she meets player 5 of the opposing team.

When the scorer is standing next to player 5 of the opposing team (who remains seated), read a question aloud for them to answer. If the jammer answers first, she scores a point, walks forward to player 4, and repeats the same process. She has a chance to defeat all five players and score five points.

If player 5 answers the question first, however, the jam period ends and no points are scored. The jammer returns to her seat and two different jammers are asked to stand and begin a new jam period.

At this time, a substitute may be inserted into the lineup for any of the starters. Substitutions should be made mandatory, so everyone will have the opportunity to play. To ensure that no one girl does all of the scoring (player 1) or original defending (player 5), the players should

change their seating order often. This will allow all of them to be jammers or defenders at some time in the game.

When the girls' six-minute period is over, the boys' period commen-
ces. The same rules apply in both the girls' and boys' periods.

When the game is over, the total number of points for each team is
totaled, and the team with more points is declared the winner.

CONCENTRATION

OBJECTIVE: To match cards and ultimately to uncover the mystery
saying.

HOW TO PLAY: On the bulletin board pin twenty (or any other number)
cards numbered from 1 to 20. Compile a list of ten pairs of matching
phrases from the lesson. Write them on the backs of the twenty cards
in jumbled order, one phrase per card.

o 1	o 5	o 9	o 13	o 17
o 2	o 6	o 10	o 14	o 18
o 3	o 7	o 11	o 15	o 19
o 4	o 8	o 12	o 16	o 20

O ADVANTAGES OF FEDERAL- ISM	O PREAMBLE	O CHECKS AND BALANCES	O 26 AMEND- MENTS	O JUDICIAL REVIEW
O CHANGES IN THE ORIGINAL CONSTI- TUTION	O SEPARATION OF POWERS	O OUTLINES ORDER AND POWERS OF GOVERN- MENT	O FIRST 10 AMEND- MENTS	O REPUBLI- CAN FORM OF GOVERN- MENT
O 7 ARTICLES	O BILL OF RIGHTS	O DISADVAN- TAGES OF FEDERAL- ISM	O POWER TO DECLARE LAWS UNCONSTI- TUTIONAL	O 3 DIFFERENT BRANCHES ARE CREATED
O AVOIDS CONCEN- TRATION OF POWER	O ONE BRANCH CAN HOLD OTHERS IN CHECK	O ANNOUNCES THE NEW GOVERN- MENT	O A REPRE- SENTATIVE GOVERN- MENT	O INVOLVES DISPUTES OVER POWER

The object of Concentration is to uncover the matches among the various cards. Begin the game by asking a student to pick two numbers. Turn over the two cards that the student requests.

If the words on the back have no relationship to each other, turn them back to the numbered side and let the next student ask for two new numbers.

If the two cards match, ask the student what they have in common. When the discussion ends (at this time students should be taking notes), remove those two cards from the board, thus exposing a portion of a mystery saying. See the illustration on the next page of the exposed portion of the saying when two cards are removed.

W	5	9	13	17
2	6	10	14	18
3	7	11	15	19
$\begin{array}{r}30\\-26\end{array}$	8	12	16	20

The student who made the match has an opportunity to guess the mystery saying. If the student declines to guess or if he guesses incorrectly, another student has a chance to match other cards.

Play continues, with matches being made and cards being removed, until someone uncovers the mystery saying. See the next page for the mystery saying for this sample game.

Two students can compete against one another in front of the class, each student can compete against all others, or the class can be divided into two teams.

CONSTRUCTION: Cut twenty cards (or as many as needed) of equal size that will fit on your bulletin board when placed in proper order. Use stiff poster board that does not bend easily. Punch a hole at the top of each card, equidistant from each side. This will enable you to remove and return the cards easily when they are pinned to the bulletin board.

On one side of each card write a number from 1 to 20 (or to correspond with the number of cards you cut) using a felt-tip pen. On the back sides of these cards write the twenty phrases in scrambled order.

To begin setting up in the classroom, staple a sheet of construction paper to the bulletin board and write a rebus on it. Finally, pin the cards, numbers facing out, to the bulletin board so that the rebus is completely covered. You are now ready to play.

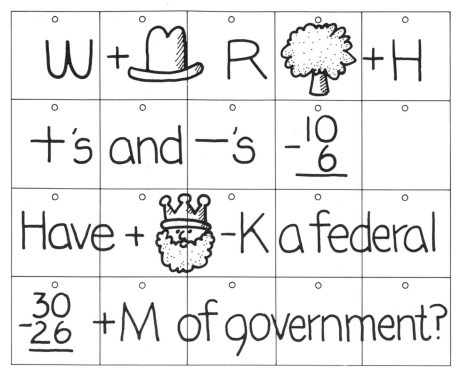

Mystery saying: "What are three plusses and minuses
for having a federal form of government?"

EYE GUESS

OBJECTIVE: To memorize positions of answers, to match answers with questions, and to score more points than the opponent.

HOW TO PLAY: This game involves two competing students who sit at the front of the room facing a bulletin board and chalkboard. The remainder of the class watches and takes notes on material covered in the course of the game. The two players might be selected on the basis of previous test scores, or any other criteria you choose.

Hang a chalkboard on the left and cover it partially by a film screen or wall map. To the right hang the bulletin board and pin eight numbered and one "eye guess" cards on it. See the illustration of this arrangement on the next page.

Play begins when you announce that the two players will now have seven seconds (or any selected time limit) to try to memorize the positions of the various answers. Raise the film screen or wall map to reveal the answers. After the time limit has expired, pull the screen or

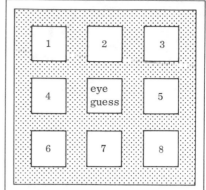

Answers hidden by map or screen

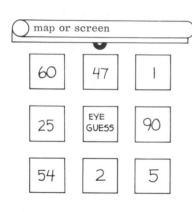
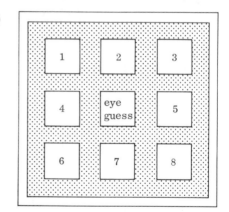

Answers revealed

map down again to hide the answers. The answers on the chalkboard are in the same position that they are on the back of the numbered cards on the bulletin board. The reason for the duplication is that, by using the chalkboard and map or screen to visually memorize the positions of the answers, the answers can be revealed and concealed simultaneously with one pull of the screen or map.

The teacher then asks the first student a question whose answer is written on one of the cards under the screen. The student then has ten seconds to try to remember the position of the answer and call for the appropriately numbered card.

Let's suppose the first student was asked how many years one must live in the state of California in order to qualify to vote. If he knew that the answer was one year, he would try to remember where he saw the number 1. If he could remember that it was in the upper right-hand corner of the diagram on the chalkboard, he would request card 3 on the bulletin board, because it corresponds to the position of the answer on the chalkboard.

Turn over the requested card and show it to the class. If the first student found the correct answer, remove that card from the bulletin board and discard the question. The student wins one point and is given a new question.

If the first student fails to match the question with a correct answer, turn back the card on the bulletin board to the numbered side, place the question at the bottom of the stack of questions, and ask the other competitor a new question.

Play proceeds until all nine questions have been matched with the nine answers (these include the eight answers behind the numbered cards and the one answer that was never exposed behind the "eye guess" card). The player who has five or more points is declared the winner.

To simulate the television version of Eye Guess as closely as possible, the teacher might allow the winner to play a reward round. Nine cards are used and marked as for the previous game completed (1, 2, 3, 4, eye guess, 5, 6, 7, 8). Various rewards are listed on the back of eight of these cards (two extra points on the next exam, for example), while on the back of the ninth card is written the word "STOP".

These cards are positioned in the same fashion as the other cards were. Instruct the winning student to select one of these nine cards by number or choose the "eye guess" card. If a reward card is selected, the student chooses a new card. The student continues to select cards until he picks the "STOP" card. At this point, the reward round is completed.

CONSTRUCTION: The first step in preparing this game is to select nine answers that have a common trait (all are numbers, names of people, famous quotations, and so on). Write a question for each of these answers on a separate 3" x 5" index card.

On nine 5" x 7" index cards, number the cards from 1 to 8 and write "eye guess" on the ninth card (use a dark felt-tip pen). On the back of these cards, write the various answers. Punch a hole in each of these cards, so that it is easy to pin them up on the bulletin board and take them down.

The next step is to pin the cards up, so that only the numbered side is visible. On an adjacent chalkboard, chalk in the answers in the same positions as they occur on the numbered cards.

Hang a film screen or wall map above this diagram, then pull it down.

If you want to use a reward round, make another set of cards like the first one. The only difference is that the backs of these cards will contain eight rewards and one STOP instead of answers.

HISTORINGO

OBJECTIVE: To cross out five consecutive squares vertically, horizontally, or diagonally.

HOW TO PLAY: Draw the following diagram on the chalkboard and have each student duplicate it on his own piece of paper. It should be large enough so that the words can be written legibly in each box.

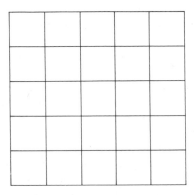

Write approximately 30 key words from the lesson on the chalkboard. Instruct the students to pick 24 of these words and write them in the boxes at random, one word per each box. Have them draw an X in the middle square. This will be a bonus space. (See illustration on next page.)

After each student has completed his card, begin the game by reading a definition or phrase that matches one of the 30 key words. For example, "anarchism" appears in one of the boxes. If you say "the system where there is no government," the student would match that phrase to the word anarchism and place an X in that box. (It is preferable to cross out the boxes in pencil. That way, the student can easily erase the X's when one game is completed and use the same card a second time.) After ten seconds have elapsed, read a second phrase aloud. Repeat this process until one student yells "historingo," signifying that he has crossed out five consecutive squares vertically, horizontally, or diagonally. Check his card by asking him to read to the class the words that he crossed out. If the check shows the student to be correct, he wins the game. Have the students erase their X's and begin a new game using the same card, this time, allowing them only five seconds between each matching phrase.

If the check reveals an error, continue playing the game but disqualify that student from that particular round. On the third round, read the phrases as rapidly as you can.

It is best to have a list of all 24 words on the card. Each time you read a definition, check off the answer. This way, you will be able to check the answers when someone calls "historingo."

NATION	SOVER-EIGNTY	POWER	GOVERN-MENT	POLITICS
STATE	ANARCHISM	AUTHORITAR-IAN SYSTEM	AUTOCRACY	OLIGARCHY
TOTALITAR-IAN SYSTEM	FEDERAL GOVERN-MENT	✕	TECHNOC-RACY	INDIRECT DEMOCRACY
ARISTOC-RACY	PRESIDEN-TIAL GOV-ERNMENT	CONFEDER-ATE GOV-ERNMENT	FIXED TERM	UNITARY GOVERN-MENT
ONE-PARTY OCRACY	THEOCRACY	PARLIA-MENTARY GOVERN-MENT	DIRECT DEMOCRACY	FEUDALISM

At the end of each game, ask if there are any questions. This will allow the students an opportunity to check the definitions that they were unable to match with the words on their cards.

JEOPARDY

OBJECTIVE: To score more points than the opposing teams by giving questions to answers.

HOW TO PLAY: Divide the class into teams of four to seven players. On a bulletin board in front of the room, arrange a set of numbered index cards under selected categories, as shown in the illustration on the next page.

Conventions	Ratification	Convention at work	Odds & Ends
1	1	1	1
2	2	2	2
3	3	3	3
4	4	4	4
5	5	5	5
6	6	6	6
7	7	7	7

The cards are punched at the top, so that when pinned to the board, they can be easily removed and returned. On the reverse side of each card is an answer in that category. As the numbers get larger, the answers become more difficult. See the illustration on the next page for sample answers in one category.

```
        o
    Odds &
    Ends
```

```
        o
    Franklin
```

```
        o
    Virginia
    Plan
```

```
        o
    New Jersey
    Plan
```

```
        o
    Taxing
    Power
```

```
        o
    Madison's
    diary
```

To begin the game, choose one student to select a category and a number. Let's suppose that the student picked the number 2 ODDS & ENDS card. You would remove the card that has been called for and read the answer on the back: Virginia Plan. At this point, any student who can think of a question to the answer Virginia Plan may raise his hand. Recognize the first student who raised his hand to verbally give a question.

If the student asks "What plan did the large states favor?", the row in which that student is seated is awarded two points and that student chooses a new card, stating the category and number. (To avoid having one student dominate the game, do not allow students to raise their hands on three consecutive answers.)

If, on the other hand, the student gives a question in which Virginia Plan is not the answer, two points are subtracted from that row's score. If that row had no points to begin with, it is now two points in the hole.

Follow this procedure until all of the cards have been removed. At this time, every row that is points ahead must send its most knowledgeable player to the front of the row with a pencil and paper.

These players may wager as many points as they desire, the maximum wager being the number of points that the row has accumulated in the game. On their piece of paper, the students secretly write the number of points being wagered. When they are ready, read a difficult answer and give them one minute to write a question to that answer on their piece of paper.

Those students who respond correctly win their bets, and their row is awarded all the wagered points. Those students who wrote a question that would not lead to the stated answer lose their bets, and their row must subtract the wagered points from their previous total. The row with the most points wins the game.

PASSWORD

OBJECTIVE: To guess the mystery word from clues given by a teammate.

HOW TO PLAY: Divide the class into two teams of equal ability. Instruct each team to select one of its members to sit in front of the class and give clues to his teammates. The two that are selected should have good vocabularies.

Acting as moderator, instruct the first person from each team to come to the front of the room and sit in front of a chalkboard, facing the class.

```
X  X  X  X  X  X  X  X          CG                |
                                          X1      |
X  X  X  X  X  X  X  X               T            |  chalk-
                                                  |  board
O  O  O  O  O  O  O  O                     O1      |
                                                  |
O  O  O  O  O  O  O  O          CG                 |
```

         CG = clue givers
    O1, X1 = players who cannot see the password
         T = teacher

Write a word that relates to the area under study on the chalkboard. Let the two clue givers view the word along with the class (except the two students with their backs to the chalkboard). Then erase the word and ask one clue giver to begin the game. He has ten seconds to give his teammate a one-word clue that is not a proper name. If either of these rules is violated, or if no clue is given in the allotted time, that team forfeits its turn. When the next clue is given, the player from the other team has ten seconds to guess the mystery word. As long as it answers correctly, a team can continue playing. This rotation of turns continues until the mystery word is guessed. The team that guessed the word is then asked to explain the significance of that word to the area under study. Any member of that team may volunteer the answer, but only one player will be recognized. If a correct answer is given, that team is awarded one point. If an incorrect answer is given, no points are awarded and the teacher explains the importance of the word.

The two players return to their seats and are replaced by the next two students.

This process continues until the end of the period or as long as interest is maintained. The team with the most points is declared the winner.

PERSONALITY

OBJECTIVE: To identify the speaker of selected quotations.

HOW TO PLAY: An opaque projector and several pictures of individuals related to the subject matter (from books, newspapers, or magazines) are needed for this game.

Darken the room and place the first picture on the opaque projector. Beside each picture place an index card with three quotations on it:

He said:

1. I have a dream.

2. Burn, baby, burn.

3. Nonviolent civil disobedience is not the answer.

One or two lines are direct quotations from the personality; the other one or two are false. Or they might all three be true or false quotations.

The teacher, without revealing the name of the person in the picture, then asks, "He said, (1) I have a dream, (2) Burn, baby, burn, or (3) Nonviolent civil disobedience is not the answer."

The students then attempt to guess what the person said. To do this, they must both be able to identify the person and know that person's philosophy.

After each picture and statement is guessed, you might briefly review that person and his philosophy for the class.

This procedure can also be used as a novel method of testing. After each picture is shown and the quotations read, instruct the students to write down the number beside the quotation(s) that they feel is (are) correct. After all the pictures and quotations have been reviewed, go over each one again and give the correct answers.

TO TELL THE TRUTH

OBJECTIVE: To question three students who claim to be the same person and to guess correctly who the "real" person is.

HOW TO PLAY: Choose three students to gather information about a person under study. Instruct them to decide among themselves who will be the two imposters and who will represent the "real" person.
   It will be the responsibility of the two impersonators to tell various, subtle lies when answering questions about themselves, while the "real" person will attempt to answer all questions correctly.
   Have the remainder of the class also do research on that personality. As they read, instruct the students to write down several questions they want to ask the individual under study.
   When everyone is ready, have the three students who claim to be the same person sit in front of the room holding cards numbered 1, 2, and 3 respectively:

X	X	X	X	X	X	X	
X	X	X	X	X	X	X	1
X	X	X	X	X	X	X	2
X	X	X	X	X	X	X	3
X	X	X	X	X	X	X	Teacher

Begin the game by stating that the three students seated at the front of the room all claim to be _____ (George Washington, for example). Then instruct the class to ask the three students about Washington's life. Through this questioning process, which should not last longer than fifteen minutes, the class members attempt to identify the two imposters through the various lies they give during the questioning period and to guess correctly who the "real" person is.
   Questions are always directed specifically at one of the three players but the same question can also be given to one of the other two. Call on students who have their hands raised to ask the questions. If there are no volunteers (which is rare), ask a question or two yourself to keep the game going.

When the questioning period is over, either because there are no more questions or because time has expired, the teacher asks the class if the real George Washington is number 1, number 2, or number 3. This can be done by a show of hands or in writing.

If you call for a show of hands, ask the class members who think number 1 is the "real" George Washington to raise their hands, and then ask a few of these students their reasons for thinking so. Repeat this process for number 2 and number 3. If the answer is given in writing, have each student list the reasons for his choice. Written answers can also be used as a homework assignment or a test; students who wrote the correct number receive credit, but those who failed to pick the "real" person receive no credit.

Either way, the game is completed when the "real" person is revealed, and a class discussion about the individual is launched. This game has proven to be an interesting and novel approach for students to study personalities in depth.

TRUTH OR CONSEQUENCES

OBJECTIVE: To tell the truth by answering questions correctly, thus avoiding the consequences of incorrect answers.

HOW TO PLAY: Compile a large set of easy questions that cover previously-learned material. Instruct the students to take out a blank sheet of paper in order to take notes on material covered in the game. Read one question aloud, then choose any student to answer it.

If the correct answer is given, that student has told the truth and a different student is selected to answer the next question.

If he gives an incorrect answer, that student must pay the consequence for not telling the truth. The consequence should, in some way, relate to the material under study (for example, if you are studying India, you might have the student sit on a small rug and attempt to make the rug fly by saying the magic words).

Continue asking questions as long as interest continues.

TWENTY QUESTIONS

OBJECTIVE: To have a student represent a person, place, or thing, and to have the class guess what the student represents by asking twenty questions or less.

HOW TO PLAY: Select a student to represent a person (such as Benjamin Franklin), place (such as Philadelphia), or thing (such as Second Continental Congress). This student must research what he is representing, so that he has a good knowledge of the topic.

When he is ready, ask the chosen student to be seated in front of the class. Acting as moderator, introduce the student to the class. Call on volunteers to ask him questions that can be answered "yes" or "no".

The game ends when a student correctly guesses what or who is being represented, or when the twenty questions have been asked. In either case, the game can lead into a class discussion of the represented person, place, or thing.

This game is an excellent semester review, when a great number of items can be represented. And because the game takes little time, it can be played several times during one period.

YOU DON'T SAY

OBJECTIVE: To guess correctly the word or name being sought through clues.

HOW TO PLAY: Divide the class into two teams. Each team selects its most able representative to come to the front of the room and give clues.

Give the two clue-givers a card with the same name written on it (George Washington Carver, for example). Choose one clue-giver to begin the game (the opportunity to go first will rotate with each new name).

The first clue-giver might give a clue such as this: "On Mondays, the typical housewife usually gets the family clothes and places them into a machine which cleans them. She is doing the family _____ ?" With that clue, that clue-giver's team discusses the clue and decides that the missing word is "washing". They have a short, specified amount of time to come up with the correct answer; someone will probably call out George Washington, among other names.

When time expires, the other clue-giver gives his clue (for example, "One who slices a roast or turkey is called a _____ ?") The second team has the same amount of time as the first to combine the two clues and to guess the name. Putting washing with carver, they will probably arrive at the answer, George Washington Carver.

The team that guesses the word or name is awarded a point, and the team that scores the most points is declared the winner. After each name is guessed, discuss with the class the importance of that word.

At no time may the clue-giver use any form of the word to be guessed in presenting his clue. If a team fails to comply, it loses a turn. You can vary the game by giving each team only one guess per turn, instead of allowing the players to call out several guesses in a specified time.